#Help!

Study Hacks

How Do I
Listen Well?

**Helen Cox Cannons
and Robyn Hardyman**

CHERITON
CHILDREN'S BOOKS

Please visit our website, www.cheritonchildrensbooks.com to see more of our high-quality books.

First Edition

Published in 2022 by **Cheriton Children's Books**
PO Box 7258, Bridgnorth WV16 9ET, UK

© 2022 Cherlton Children's Books

Authors: Helen Cox Cannons and Robyn Hardyman
Designer: Paul Myerscough
Editor: Jennifer Sanderson
Picture Researcher: Rachel Blount
Proofreader: Wendy Scavuzzo

Picture credits: Cover: Shutterstock/Wayhome Studio. Inside: p1: Shutterstock/Rido; p4: Shutterstock/Monkey Business Images; p5: Shutterstock/Monkey Business Images; p6: Shutterstock/Monkey Business Images; p7: Shutterstock/Monkey Business Images; p8: Shutterstock/Robert Kneschke; p9: Shutterstock/Monkey Business Images; p10: Shutterstock/SpeedKingz; p11: Shutterstock/YanLev; p12: Shutterstock/Tyler Olson; p13: Shutterstock/Monkey Business Images; p14: Shutterstock/wavebreakmedia; p15: Shutterstock/Sergey Novikov; p16: Shutterstock/Oksana Kuzmina; p17: Shutterstock/ Syda Productions; p18: Shutterstock/Syda Productions; p19: Shutterstock/Daniel M Ernst; p20: Shutterstock/michaeljung; p21: Shutterstock/VGstockstudio; p22: Shutterstock/NarongchaiHlaw; p23: Shutterstock/Monkey Business Images; p24: Shutterstock/Tyler Olson; p25: Shutterstock/arrowsmith2; p26: Shutterstock/ Gorodenkoff; p27: Shutterstock/Rido; p28: Shutterstock/Monkey Business Images; p29: Shutterstock/Drazen Zigic.

Printed in the United States of America

Contents

Help! Why Should I Listen?

#Help! You're in class and your teacher is talking and talking (about homework—again!). You just want to get to lunch and hang out with your friends! But hold on—here's why you should listen. Being able to listen well is a great skill. And with some simple tips, it is one that is easy—and fun—to learn.

#Hack: Listening well makes your time in class go much faster!

Listening Is for Life!

Before we learn tips on listening, let's find out why being able to listen well is so important. Hearing is a **passive** activity. Our ears receive sounds without us trying to hear them. But listening is **active**. We choose what we listen and pay attention to (like instructions to wash the dishes!). Listening is one of the most important tools for learning. It is also an important life skill. Good listening is at the heart of all our understanding and at the center of our **communication** with others.

It is important to listen to instructions when you are playing team sports.

What's So Great About Listening?

You need to listen carefully to gain knowledge and understanding. But why would you want to listen at all? These are the benefits of being an active listener:

- You'll learn a lot! Much of what you are taught is explained **verbally**, by your teachers. If you pay attention to what you hear, you will learn more.
- You'll get to join in! If you listen carefully to the ideas and opinions of others, you will be able to engage in interesting discussions with the speaker.
- You will be able to remember so much more! The more you listen, the more you **concentrate**. The more you concentrate, the better your memory skills. It's simple!
- You'll make friends! Everyone loves a good listener. If people think you understand them, they'll want to talk to you.
- You can keep safe. It can be dangerous not to listen. Instructions and warnings are often spoken to us.

Chapter One
Help! How Do I Pay Attention?

#ListenUp! OK, let's admit it—having to listen all day at school can feel really tough. However, whether your principal, teacher, or a classmate is talking, you need to listen! These top tips will help you listen **effectively**, no matter who the speaker is. Remember, the better you listen, the more you will learn. Did anyone say Grade A?!

Sit Up to Listen Up!

A key to listening well is to pay attention to the person who is speaking. Engaging with a person means **focusing** fully on what that person is saying and doing. You need to engage physically as well as mentally to listen well. Before a lesson begins, make sure you can see and hear the person talking. That makes it much easier for you to focus on them and to concentrate. Sitting up in your chair can be a good way to keep yourself alert.

Try to position yourself so you can see the speaker well.

You Can Hack It!

Sitting upright in class can help you listen better. Can you think of other situations in which good **posture** might help improve your concentration?

#Help!

How Do I Listen Well?

Remember that, to listen properly, you need to pay attention to the speaker. Try these top listening tips:

- *Sit away from windows and doors:* Unwanted noise might reach you from outside the classroom.
- *If you can, face the speaker directly:* Try to sit with your front facing them.
- *Make yourself comfortable:* Be sure you are not too hot or too cold so you are not **distracted**.

How Do I Deal with Distractions?

Finding it hard to focus? Yup, it's a problem. That's because there are always sounds and sights to distract us. When you need to pay attention to information from a speaker, or when you need to focus on your schoolwork, one listening tip is to make sure you are not distracted.

Hey, Is Anyone Home?!...

Most people find that their mind tends to wander from time to time. To help you focus only on what you are listening to, try to remove things that can distract you. Different things distract different people. Some people are distracted by other people talking. Others can't help looking out the window, or thinking about what they will eat for dinner! Distractions such as these keep you from focusing on what a speaker is saying. To avoid distractions, create a peaceful and focused frame of mind—so you are ready to listen. It's a good idea to ask your fellow listeners to do the same. That way, you will all help each other.

#Hack: Put your cell phone away. They are not allowed in classes for good reason!

I'm All Ears!

You will also listen well if you decide you are ready and willing to listen and learn. Before you go to class, try to make the effort to find out about the day's topic—and to find it interesting. You'll be amazed what a difference a positive attitude will make to your listening. It will put you in the right frame of mind to concentrate and gain knowledge.

It is easier to stay focused and to listen well when everyone around you is listening, too.

How Do I Stay Focused?

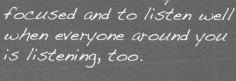

Remember that effective listening requires quiet concentration. Try to follow these simple tips to be sure your listening is focused:

- Sit by quiet people who will not talk while you are trying to listen. And avoid those people who distract you (you know who they are!).
- Be **committed**. Effective listening takes effort.

Chapter Two
Help! How Do I Listen in a Group?

#WhatDoYouThink? Discussions are an important part of group learning. You may be **debating** a topic in small groups or one-on-one. Sometimes, the whole class might join in, led by the teacher. In all these situations, it's important to listen to what other people are saying. If you listen to other people, you can think about their opinions. You can then respond.

I Hear You!

Effective listening in discussions begins with everyone having an open mind. This means being ready and willing to consider what other people have to say, even if you think you are going to disagree with them. Try to come to a debate ready to hear new information, ideas, and points of view. You will be more active in your listening if you try to avoid having fixed ideas about a topic. It's fine to have some knowledge and information of your own. However, do not **assume** that is the only knowledge there is. You may not always be right about something! Keeping an open mind takes practice.

It's important to listen to everyone's opinion in discussions.

Try to go into the classroom with an open mind, ready to learn.

Mind Made Up?

If you come to a discussion with your mind already made up, you are more likely to have an **agenda** of your own for the discussion. That means you will be determined to put forward your own ideas and not consider others. You may plan to **convince** others of your viewpoint, or to speak most often. However, having an agenda will not help you, or others, learn.

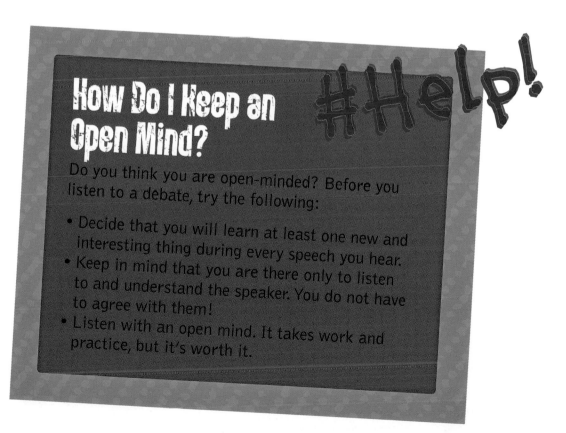

How Do I Keep an Open Mind? #Help!

Do you think you are open-minded? Before you listen to a debate, try the following:

• Decide that you will learn at least one new and interesting thing during every speech you hear.
• Keep in mind that you are there only to listen to and understand the speaker. You do not have to agree with them!
• Listen with an open mind. It takes work and practice, but it's worth it.

How Do I Use My Ears and Eyes?

Did you know that you use your eyes when you listen? Yes, you read that right! It's not just your ears that need to do the work. It's much easier to focus on what someone is saying if you look at them. Here are some tips on how to use your eyes as well as your ears to listen effectively.

Sloppy Sitting = Sloppy Listening

If you slouch in your chair and look at the floor while someone is talking, you may easily get distracted. Try to be **attentive** in your body language. Sit up straight and look directly at the person speaking to you. Wherever you focus your eyes, your brain will follow. Continue to look at the speaker until they have finished talking.

#Hack: Try not to slouch on your desk. You might fall asleep in class!

See the Signs (They're Out There!)

Speakers may also give you clues to help with your listening. Listen for changes in the pace of their speech. They may slow down when they want to **emphasize** an important point. They may also repeat key information points. Watch the way they move around, or use their hands for emphasis. Also watch how they use their notes. They may use them more when communicating details, or examples. That's a cue for you to listen particularly carefully.

Keep your eyes focused on the teacher as much as possible.

How Can I Be a Listening Detective? #Help!

Try to use your senses of sight and hearing when you listen to a person speak. That will help you notice any clues the speaker gives as they talk. Here are some key listening tips to follow to make sure you follow all the clues a speaker gives:

- *Keep your eyes on the speaker*: This direct line of contact will help you concentrate.
- *Watch for change*: Look for changes in the pace and volume of the speaker's speech.
- *Look for the signs*: Watch for clues in the speaker's behavior.

How Do I Get Ready to Talk?

Are you super organized and always ready for class? Or do you just go with the flow? Well, preparation is an important part of learning. When you are having a class or group discussion, try to do some preparation work beforehand. If you already have some knowledge of a topic, it will be easier for you to listen and take in what your teachers or classmates are saying.

Ready with Research

Before you come to class, read and study any materials you have been given beforehand. Find out as much as you can about the topic. **Research** the different opinions about your topic. Understanding that there is more than one point of view will help you to be an active listener. And knowing as much as possible about the topic will help you to **evaluate** what you hear.

#Hack: Researching a topic with your friends can be more fun than going it alone.

You Can Hack It!

Which of your classes do you think you could prepare for more effectively?

One Step Ahead

Active listeners productively use the information they learn before a talk or discussion. If you have researched your topic, you will find it easier to concentrate as you listen to the speaker. You will not have to waste time trying to grasp the topic. That means you will have more time to take in new information and think about what is being said. If you are part of a group in a discussion, try to share what you have learned so far with the other members of your group.

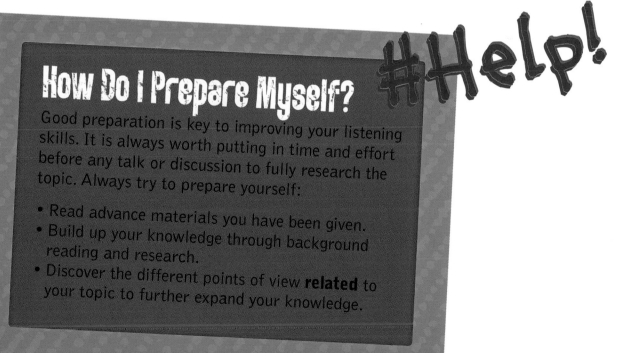

How Do I Prepare Myself? #Help!

Good preparation is key to improving your listening skills. It is always worth putting in time and effort before any talk or discussion to fully research the topic. Always try to prepare yourself:

- Read advance materials you have been given.
- Build up your knowledge through background reading and research.
- Discover the different points of view **related** to your topic to further expand your knowledge.

How Do I Use My Brain?

Your brain is the powerhouse of your body. And at your age, your brain is reaching its peak! To make the best use of your intelligence, you need to be able to concentrate and focus on information. When you concentrate, you can fully take in what is being said and your amazing brain will start to make **connections** with what you have already learned.

Super Thinker

You can listen to and understand language around two or three times faster than a person can speak. That means you have a lot of spare **capacity** in your brain to think about other things while we you are listening. The downside to that super smartness is that you can get easily distracted! A good listener knows how to use the spare capacity in their brain to think about what the speaker is saying.

If you listen carefully your brain will make connections with what you already know.

Focusing on a speaker is an important skill in the workplace.

Engage the Brain!

If you are listening to a classmate in a discussion, try to think about how their viewpoint would work in practice. Follow the details of the argument, and test it out. Use what you already know to help you test the viewpoint. Ask yourself the following questions: Is the argument clear? Does it agree with what you already know or think? If not, could you be mistaken? How can you explore the topic further in your debate? By questioning the speaker's viewpoint as you listen to them, you will remain focused on what they are saying.

#Help!

How Do I Make Connections?

Now that you know your mind can become easily distracted, you can keep it in check! Remember that active listeners make connections. Try to follow these steps to make sure you stay focused on the discussion and listen to every word the speaker says:

- *Keep connecting*: Link what you are hearing to what you already know.
- *Think carefully*: Examine the speaker's viewpoint.
- *Question*: Ask yourself whether you agree with the viewpoint, and how you can move the discussion forward.

Chapter Three
Help! How Do I Listen Politely?

#Manners! OK, so you are concentrating on listening to the speaker. You're getting really interested. In fact, you really want to ask some questions. And you want to know the answers—right now! You may want to raise your hand to get the speaker's attention and ask your questions. Try to hold back, though. It's important to keep quiet and let the speaker finish. Let's learn how to listen politely.

Wait for It!

It is a courtesy to let a speaker finish their talk. They have something to say, and you should stay quiet while they are talking. Your mind may be racing, but try to just listen. You might miss something important if you speak up too soon. Often speakers make a useful summary at the end of their speech, or they save the most important material until the end. They will have thought about how to **structure** their speech—and often keep the best for last!

If you interrupt a speaker before they have finished their talk, they may forget to tell the audience something important.

Don't Jump In!

It is tempting to jump in, when you are really engaged with the topic, but try not to interrupt. Don't finish the speaker's sentences for them, and don't call out, "I knew that!" or "But…" Don't even speak up to agree with the speaker. Just listen! Your role is not to show how smart you are, but to listen and understand. Your turn to speak will come.

A speaker may get mad if you interrupt them. Try to listen to the speaker and don't interrupt—even if you really disagree strongly!

How Do I Hold Back and Keep Quiet?

#Help!

Remember that effective listeners stay quiet until the speaker has finished. Work on being patient and calm throughout a talk, saving your questions until the very end when you know that the speaker has finished talking. Try to keep these courtesy points in mind as you listen:

- Don't interrupt, even to agree with the speaker.
- If the speaker is arguing against your opinion, let them make their point. You will know the whole argument, and be able to respond better at the end of the talk.
- Your role is simply to listen—that way you will be able to understand what the speaker is saying.

How Do I Speak Up?

You've listened and you've learned. The speaker has finished their talk, and is open to answering any questions you or your classmates might have. Now is your chance to think about your response to the speaker's thoughts, ideas, and opinions. Great—you've got a whole pile of things to say! But hold on, there are ways to speak up with style...

So What Do You Think?

Do you agree or disagree with the speaker? That is the point when you bring together everything you learned before the talk along with everything you have heard the speaker say. Using your previous knowledge, and having listened attentively, you can now make up your mind about the speaker's presentation. Consider your response before speaking. Did the speaker add new information or **insight** that changed your viewpoint? Is your mind honestly open to being changed?

Think carefully about everything that the speaker has to say.

How Can I Think Before I Speak?

Remember that good listeners think before they respond. Before you jump in with questions and opinions, take some time to work through your thoughts:

- Keep an open mind while you **review** the speaker's ideas. Try to curb your immediate reactions.
- Consider the ideas together with all the **evidence** provided by the speaker.
- Relate the speaker's evidence and ideas to what you learned before the talk.
- Respond when you are invited to, calmly and with **authority**.

Keep to the Point

It's a good idea to stop yourself from speaking up immediately after a talk has finished. Wait a little while before you jump in. It's tempting to speak first and speak loudest, but your first reaction may not be the best one. You will make a better contribution to the discussion if you think first, and talk later. Your response will then be on-target and will **elaborate** on what has already been said.

You Can Hack It!

Why do you think a speaker will appreciate you asking questions that show you have listened to what they had to say?

How Do I Ask Questions?

So you've had a good chance to think about what the speaker said. If you have listened carefully, there is a good chance you have thought of some intelligent questions. But how do you go about asking them? These tips will help you to ask effective questions that make a good contribution toward class discussion.

Ask the Right Questions

The point of listening is to understand. You need to check your understanding by asking yourself questions. That may not always be easy, but don't just give up and stop listening when the information is difficult. When the subject is hard to understand, you need to listen even more carefully. Asking questions is a sign of intelligent listening. The key is to ask the right questions, and to also ask them well.

Let's Clear Things Up

If there are words you do not understand, make a note to ask about their meaning. Others in class will almost certainly not have understood the words either. It helps to clarify the speaker's argument if you ask questions such as, "So is it correct that you are saying…?" If the speaker's point is not clear to you, you could ask "Can you give me an example of…?" Be sure to ask questions, rather than just stating your own opinion.

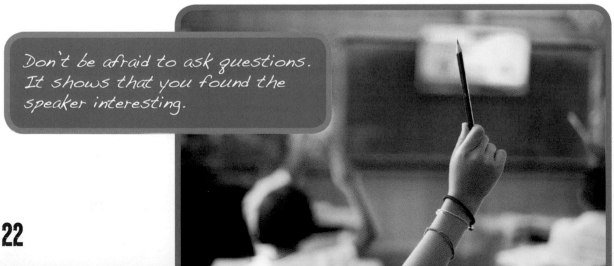

Don't be afraid to ask questions. It shows that you found the speaker interesting.

#Hack: If you don't understand something, ask the speaker and they will explain it to you.

#Help!

What Questions Should I Ask?

Asking questions after a talk is one of the most effective listening tools you can use. If you have listened well to everything the speaker had to say, you will be prepared to ask **relevant** questions. Before you direct your questions to the speaker, try to remember these points:

• First **paraphrase** the point the speaker made, to ensure you have understood them correctly.
• Ask questions about details of vocabulary or meaning.
• Don't be afraid to ask questions—everyone will gain value from them.
• Try to keep your questions relevant and do not go off the topic.
• Do not try to impress or **influence** the speaker. The aim of your questions should be to clarify the speaker's meaning.

Chapter Four

Help! How Do I Make Sense?

#MyHeadHurts! There's so much new information in your brain—it feels like it's going to explode! What do you do with all this knowledge? And what does it all mean? It's very important to be able to clarify, or make sense of, the information you have heard. You need to listen well to be able to work through the words being said to you, so you can become a truly active listener.

Here's How to Do It

As with all listening activities, to improve your comprehension, you need to engage with the speaker, decide to concentrate, and make connections with what you hear. However, your task is to understand and summarize, not to respond. Your own reaction to the text is not important here. You are not required to evaluate and ask questions about a point of view presented by the speaker.

Summarizing information and being able to write it down accurately is an awesome life skill.

*When watching a **factual** program in class, make note of any questions you may have.*

Huh? What Is That?!

If you are listening to factual information, such as a film or TV program in class, check that you understand the vocabulary. If you are not sure of the meaning of a word, think about the **context** in which it is being used. That will help you understand the word. If you are still not sure, ask what the word means at the end of the showing or look up the meaning in a dictionary. If you are listening to a reading of fictional text, such as a novel or play, it can also help to visualize what you hear, to make pictures of it in your head.

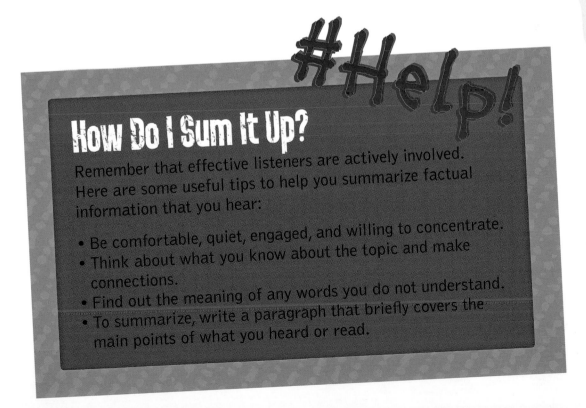

#Help!

How Do I Sum It Up?

Remember that effective listeners are actively involved. Here are some useful tips to help you summarize factual information that you hear:

- Be comfortable, quiet, engaged, and willing to concentrate.
- Think about what you know about the topic and make connections.
- Find out the meaning of any words you do not understand.
- To summarize, write a paragraph that briefly covers the main points of what you heard or read.

How Do I Take Notes?

Do your fingers ever ache from writing so much?! Writing notes is a constant part of school life. But writing is also an important skill that you need to master throughout your life. Whether you are taking notes from a conversation or summarizing information from a speaker, you need to be able to listen, **identify** the key points, and write them down.

What's the Point?

When listening to a speaker in a discussion, you need to identify each point they make. You also need to know how they support each point with evidence. If you can take short notes about points and evidence while the speaker is talking, that will show you the structure of their argument. It will also highlight any gaps in the presentation, or in your understanding.

Don't Write It All Down!

Taking notes is also a key skill when listening to a speaker. Remember to follow the speaker's words carefully and take notes. However, you cannot write as fast as the speaker can speak! Taking notes requires you to carefully choose what to write, which requires active listening. Remember, you are **processing** what you hear and deciding what is important.

You Can Hack It!

Why do you think taking notes while the speaker talks could help you ask relevant questions?

When taking notes, try to carefully listen to everything the speaker says.

#Help!

How Do I Take Good Notes?

Note-taking is very important—it will be a record of the most important things you have listened to during a discussion or talk. Remember these key tips for awesome note-taking:

- When a point is made in a discussion, listen for the supporting evidence. Make a note of the point and the evidence.
- Write quickly. The notes are only for your own use and don't have to be neat.
- Make a quick note of your follow-up questions and any words that you do not understand.
- When an **informational** text is read aloud, write down the main ideas.

Help! How Do I Listen for Life?

#ListeningIsForLife! So, you've learned how to listen well in school. But you also need to listen well at home and when you are out and about. Whether you're making new friends, listening to instructions on a day out, or listening to your favorite music, improving your listening skills can improve your life. Here's why you should love listening for life!

Listen to Your Family (Yes, Really!)

Good listening is a life skill that will help you in many ways. At home, listen to your family members. Practice that when you sit at the table during meals. Perhaps there are things you didn't know about your family history. You could try asking your grandparents what life was like when they were young. When you are with your friends, try to let one person speak at a time. If a friend is in trouble, try to listen to them without interrupting. That will show you support them.

Listen to your family—they are probably more interesting than you think!

Keep Going!

Like any skill, good listening takes practice. Everyone finds that their mind wanders sometimes. With practice, you will learn when that is most likely to happen to you. You'll then be able to check yourself, and get your active listening back on track.

Listen, You're a Natural!

After a while, you won't need to use tools such as charts while listening. With a lot of listening practice, you will start to listen effectively with little effort. You can then gain more knowledge and understanding. You will have become a great listener!

And finally—great listening leads to great marks. What's not to love?!

#Help!

How Can I Remember How to Listen?

A chart can be a useful tool that will remind you of the steps involved in active listening. Include the following points on your chart:

- Be prepared.
- Engage with the speaker.
- Remove distractions.
- Decide to concentrate.
- Make connections with what you know.
- Let the speaker finish talking.
- Ask questions.

Glossary

active something that we do with intentional thought

agenda a plan or goal that guides one's behavior, and is often kept secret

assume to accept that something is the case without any proof or evidence

attentive paying close attention to something

authority having knowledge from a reliable source

capacity the amount that something can hold or someone can do

committed having made a decision to do something

communication the exchange of information with another person

concentrate give your full attention or effort to something

connections links between one thing and another

context the background to the way something is said, which helps to explain it

convince to persuade someone that something is true or correct

debating exchanging opinions

distracted having your attention drawn away from something

effectively with a good result, well

elaborate explain in more detail

emphasize give special importance to something

evaluate to think about the importance of something

evidence facts or objects used to support the truth of something

factual based on real events

focusing concentrating on something

identify recognize something and pay attention to it

influence to affect or alter something to make it different

informational providing factual information

insight being able to understand the truth about something

paraphrase to use different words to describe the meaning of a text

passive something we do not take an active part in

posture the position in which someone holds their body

processing thinking carefully about

related connected to something else

relevant meaningful to a topic

research find out about something

review go over again

structure how something is arranged

verbally spoken, not written

Find Out More

Books

Daniels, Natasha. *Social Skills Activities for Kids: 50 Fun Exercises for Making Friends, Talking and Listening, and Understanding Social Rules.* Rockridge Press, 2019.

Rashid, Imran. *Offline: Free Your Mind from Smartphone and Social Media Stress.* Capstone Publishing, 2018.

Sherman, Hannah. *Mindfulness Workbook for Kids.* Callisto Media, 2020.

Websites

Discover more tools and techniques for listening and other study skills at:
http://kidshealth.org/kid/homework/classwork/studying. html#cat20953

Learn more about how to effectively take part in classroom discussions:
www.theclassroom.com/debating-skills-children-8308213.html

Find out how to stay focused in the classroom at:
www.wikihow.com/Pay-Attention-in-Class

Publisher's note to educators and parents:

All the websites featured above have been carefully reviewed to ensure that they are suitable for students. However, many websites change often, and we cannot guarantee that a slte's future contents will continue to meet our high standards of educational value. Please be advised that students should be closely monitored whenever they access the Internet.

Index

About the Authors

Helen Cox Cannons and Robyn Hardyman are wonderful authors who have written many children's information books on a huge variety of subjects, including why it is so important to listen well!